P9-CDZ-267

A Young Citizen's Guide to News Literacy

THE IMPORTANCE OF GOOD SOURCES

Lisa A. McPartland

PowerKiDS
press.
New York

Published in 2019 by The Rosen Publishing Group, Inc.
29 East 21st Street, New York, NY 10010

First Edition

Editor: Jill Keppeler
Book Design: Reann Nye

Photo Credits: Cover DreamPictures/The Image Bank/Getty Images; p. 5 Petri Oeschger/Moment/ Getty Images; p. 6 wavebreakmedia/Shutterstock.com; p. 7 Africa Studio/Shutterstock.com; p. 8 Mihajlo Maricic/EyeEm/Getty Images; p. 9 bonniej/E+/Getty Images; p. 11 BigTunaOnline/Shutterstock.com; p. 12 AngleStudio/Shutterstock.com; p. 13 fizkes/Shutterstock.com; p. 15 NikoEndres/Shutterstock.com; p. 17 GaudiLab/Shutterstock.com; p. 19 PeopleImages/DigitalVision/Getty Images; p. 21 DW labs Incorporated/Shutterstock.com; p. 23 Surapol Usanakul/Shutterstock.com; p. 25 Yellow Dog Productions Inc./Photodisc/Getty Images; pp. 27, 28, 30 wavebreakmedia/Shutterstock.com; p. 29 Gary Burchell/ Taxi/Getty Images.

Cataloging-in-Publishing Data

Names: McPartland, Lisa A.
Title: The importance of good sources / Lisa A. McPartland.
Description: New York : PowerKids Press, 2019. | Series: A young citizen's guide to news literacy | Includes glossary and index.
Identifiers: ISBN 9781538346143 (pbk.) | ISBN 9781538345016 (library bound) | ISBN 9781538346150 (6 pack)
Subjects: LCSH: Journalistic ethics–Juvenile literature. | Journalism–Objectivity–Juvenile literature. | Journalism–Juvenile literature.
Classification: LCC PN4797.M43 2019 | DDC 174'.907–dc23

Manufactured in the United States of America

CPSIA Compliance Information: Batch #CWPK19: For Further Information contact Rosen Publishing, New York, New York at 1-800-237-9932

CONTENTS

WHAT IS A SOURCE?

If you wanted to learn how to stay healthy, which person would you ask? Would you ask a friend, the person who cuts your hair, or your doctor? Before you decide, you would probably ask yourself, "Who would be a good source for this information?"

A source is any person, thing, or place from which you obtain something. It's important to consider good sources of information when you have questions. It's also important to consider sources in the news you read, watch, or listen to. When you read news articles or stories on websites or watch or listen to news broadcasts, how do you tell who and what the sources of information are? How do you know a **journalist** is using good sources?

When you're reading, how do you know what information is good or bad? We'll explore how to tell the difference between good and bad sources of information.

GOOD INFORMATION

You probably guessed that a doctor is the best source for information about staying healthy. In fact, it's a doctor's job to help you stay healthy! You go to see a doctor to make sure you're well or to find out how to get better if you're sick.

Other people could probably give you tips about health, but if they're not trained in real medicine, the information might not be good. Your friend also could tell you their ideas, but those ideas will probably be similar to what you already know. This example also can be applied to the news. How do journalists decide what makes a source a good source? A good source is one that is **credible**, trustworthy, and timely. A good source also knows a lot about the subject.

Who would know the most about staying healthy? Doctors go to school to learn about health and medicine.

There are many examples of good sources that news reporters can use. Reporters begin by interviewing people who have firsthand experience with the topics of their stories. This means that the sources have witnessed the events or that the sources know a lot about the topic. If a reporter is working on a story about a crime, they might talk to someone who witnessed it or a police officer who's working on the case. They wouldn't want to talk to someone who just has a guess about it!

Experts on a topic may be good sources for information. Other good sources include books or journals written by respected authors and websites created by credible groups. Hospitals, schools, or government agencies may have websites that are good sources.

There are many things to consider when you're figuring out if a source is a good source. A reporter begins by interviewing people who are connected to a story. They may have witnessed an event or know a lot about the topic.

PRIMARY AND SECONDARY SOURCES

Sources may be primary or secondary. Primary sources provide facts about events, objects, or people. Written materials can be primary sources if the people who experienced the events at the time wrote them. Books, magazines, newspaper stories, photographs, and blogs may be primary sources. Secondary sources describe primary sources and are written a while after the events. Secondary sources include reference books, textbooks, history books, or writings that offer criticism.

ALL SORTS OF SOURCES

Even beyond those sources, there are many different ways to get information. In addition to websites, other electronic sources of information include emails, video and sound recordings, and social network posts and messages (such as those on Facebook, Twitter, and Instagram). Even works of art and music can be considered sources.

It's clear that information comes in many forms. It's important to be able to tell the difference between good sources and bad sources so you can tell if the news and information you're reading, watching, or listening to is true. For example, a tweet might tell you something about what a person thinks, but would you want to trust it for facts? That's probably not a good idea! You'd want to get more information first.

BREAKING NEWS

Tools, coins, cars, items of clothing, furniture, and other objects may be good primary sources of information about the past. These objects are called artifacts.

Be very cautious about information you
see online. What's the source?

11

THINK ABOUT IT

In the earlier example, we decided that the doctor was a good source of information because it's a doctor's job to deal with health problems. Doctors are experts on health and medicine. The person who cuts your hair would be a good source of information if you had questions about hair care, not if you wanted to learn about staying healthy. And your friend might think eating a lot of candy is great for you! They might have reasons to want to believe that.

If you can identify good sources in something you see on television or read in a newspaper or on a website, then you'll know the story contains good information and that you can trust it. It's also good to consider a source's motive. Why are they providing information?

Sometimes people share information because they want you to do something or feel a certain way. If you find yourself getting angry, think about why!

13

For example, say you read two articles a friend told you about. In one, the reporter talked to a doctor who said that eating too much candy isn't very good for you, but a little candy is fine. You look up the doctor's name online and she's a real doctor. She went to a real medical school, graduated with a medical degree, and has an office in your city where she sees patients.

In the other article, no reporter's name is listed. The person quoted in the article says he's a doctor, but he also says eating all the candy you want is good for you. You look up his name online and see that he doesn't really seem to be a doctor. But he does own a candy store! What story can you trust?

BREAKING NEWS

Ethical reporters are **accountable** and transparent. This means they are clear about their sources, respond quickly to questions, and admit to and correct mistakes.

If something seems too good to be true—maybe it is! Candy may be tasty, but eating a lot of it isn't good for you.

BEING MEDIA LITERATE

It's important for news consumers to be **media literate**. Here are some questions that you can ask to **evaluate** information:

- Who created the message?
- What **techniques** are used to get my attention?
- How might different people interpret the message?
- Did someone pay for this? Who?
- What points of view and values are in the message? Was anything left out, and why?
- Why is this message being sent?

ANONYMOUS SOURCES

If a good source is a source that's credible, trustworthy, timely, and reliable, then a bad source is the opposite. A bad news source may also be one that shares opinions, rumors, or **biased** information. They might not be able to back up what they're saying with facts.

Reporters sometimes use anonymous, or unnamed, sources. This is because sometimes sources will speak only if they're not named in news stories. They might do this because they're worried they'll get in trouble. However, there are risks with anonymous sources. People can't decide if they trust a source if they don't know who the source is or what their motive might be. A journalist should explain why the source is anonymous in the story so people can decide what they think.

BREAKING NEWS

According to some journalism ethics codes, a journalist should allow a source to remain anonymous only if the source faces harm and only if the source has information no one else can provide.

A source might wish to stay anonymous because they could get in trouble. For example, an employee of a company that's polluting the environment might speak to a reporter about the problem—but they could lose their job if their boss finds out about it!

DOMAIN SUFFIX

A domain suffix, the end of a website address, provides clues about who created a website. Some of the more common domain suffixes are:
- .com—a commercial website
- .edu—a website for an educational institution, such as a school or a college
- .gov—a website created by a government agency
- .org—a website operated by a nonprofit group

Not all websites are reliable. In fact, many are not! Wikipedia isn't a good source because it can be edited by anyone.

FACTS, OPINIONS, AND RUMORS

One way young readers or viewers can determine if a reporter used good sources is by studying news items to see if they contains facts, opinions, or rumors. A fact is a detail that's true based on **objective** proof, such as physical or scientific evidence. A fact can be **verified** by looking at other good sources.

An opinion is a belief that can't be proven or disproven. This means an opinion can't be verified (although the facts they're based on may be proven). Be careful: people often present opinions as facts. Writers may also use opinions to persuade readers to agree with them. A rumor is a story that someone shares even though the information might not be true. Don't trust rumors! Don't trust stories with rumors, either.

BREAKING NEWS

Newspapers, news websites, and news broadcasts sometimes have opinion pieces, too. These should be clearly labeled so people don't think they're news.

Rumors can move fast! They can hurt people, too.
It's important to avoid spreading rumors.

SUBJECTIVE INFORMATION

Subjective information is the opposite of objective information. Subjective information presents one person's views on a topic, and the information can be twisted by their feelings. All opinions are subjective, but some subjective information can be backed up with facts. Words may provide clues that a source is offering subjective information. Some of these words include "all," "always," "should," and "never." If a news story uses these types of words, seek another source to verify the information.

BIASED INFORMATION

Bias is when a person shows a tendency to believe that some people or ideas are better than others. Everyone has biases, but it's important that news reporters don't show them in their stories. You can see bias when a writer uses certain facts or words to share particular opinions. Biased sources are one sided. They try to affect how people think by sharing certain pieces of information while leaving out other pieces of information.

Understanding how a source might be biased can help you decide what news sources to trust. Keep several questions in mind. Did the source leave out information? What words create positive or **negative** impressions? What would you think about this article or broadcast if the source had used different words?

BREAKING NEWS

Be aware of words that show bias and opinion. These words often are loaded with emotion. These words may include "amazing," "awful," "bad," "good," "smart," "stupid," and "very."

People quoted in news stories will have their own biases. This is different from if reporters put their own biases in a story. Stories should still present balanced views when possible, however.

WHAT IS PROPAGANDA?

Propaganda is when people spread ideas, information, or rumors for the purpose of helping or hurting someone or something. Propaganda can be based in fact, but those who spread it present facts in a certain way to get the response they want. If you read or watch something presented as fact that describes opinions or positions in terms of how good or bad they are, that source might be propaganda.

PUTTING IT TOGETHER

Let's revisit the example of staying healthy. We decided that your friend wouldn't be a good source if they believe that eating candy is a great way to stay healthy. Your friend could try to persuade you by using facts, opinions, rumors, and biased information. Your friend could tell you that candy is made of sugar and that sugar is sweet.

Both these statements are facts you can verify. You can look at the ingredients of candy and you can taste sugar. Still, it doesn't prove candy is good for you. Your friend could also tell you that candy tastes good. That's their opinion! If you like sweet treats, you may agree. If not, you might not agree. Either way, it still doesn't prove anything.

You can take what you've learned about identifying good sources and apply the lessons to what you see and read.

If your friend told you that they've heard all their other friends eat candy all day to stay healthy, that's a rumor. Even if they've heard that, it doesn't make it true! You could disprove it by asking someone who's friends with both of you. Also, you know your parents wouldn't allow you to eat candy all the time, so you could guess that other children's parents also wouldn't let them do this.

How could bias fit into this example? Your friend could say that candy is the healthiest type of food because they don't like the taste of vegetables or fruit. Also, your friend might leave out facts about other foods—such as how healthy they are compared to candy—in order to persuade you to agree with their opinions.

BREAKING NEWS

These questions can help you figure out what's fact. Can you prove the statement? Can you observe the statement happening? Can you verify the statement with witnesses or **documents**?

Your friend might not be a good source of information about staying healthy. They might not want to think candy isn't good for them, because they like it!

25

VERIFY IT

There are ways you can verify information you read or hear. Determine why someone created the story, article, post, or news broadcast. Is it in a newspaper or TV station (or on a website) with a good reputation? Does it seem to be trying to sell you something or persuade you of something? Next, check for the same information in other good sources. If more than one is reporting the same thing, that's a good sign.

Check for **accuracy** and timeliness. Do all the facts seem to add up? Is it a recent story? Consider the credibility of the person writing the story and of the sources used. If there is no author listed or if the author uses anonymous sources, consider why the author and sources weren't named.

A source is a good source if you can verify the information. Consider the steps in this chapter when determining if a source is a good source.

VERIFYING WEBSITES

Keep several things in mind when you read information on a website. Be suspicious if a website doesn't provide an author or contact information. Also, make sure the website's purpose is clear and that the author gives the sources of their information. Readers also should check for writing mistakes, misspellings, and other problems. Question the credibility of a website if you find a lot of mistakes.

SHARING THESE LESSONS

If you want to teach your family and friends how to make sure the news they're reading or watching comes from good sources, teach them to ask questions. Where was the story printed, posted, or broadcast? Is the news outlet reliable? Is the information timely? Consider if the information is fact or opinion. How can you tell? Why would someone want to post, print, or broadcast this story? Are they trying to sell you something or get you to do something?

Encouraging your family and friends to ask themselves these questions will teach them how to make sure the news they're reading, watching, or posting is true. This can also help your family and friends think more deeply about what they see in the news and on social media.

Talk to your family and friends about how to recognize good sources in print news, broadcast news, or online news. How will you share what you have learned with others?

IT'S IMPORTANT!

It's important to understand good sources because these sources can help you decide if what you're reading—in print and on the Internet—or watching should be trusted. Understanding good sources also helps you decide if stories or online posts present facts, opinions, rumors, or information that's biased. You can teach your family and friends to verify information when they're reading the news and information on websites or social media.

It's important to ask questions and teach your family and friends to ask questions. If something seems too good or too weird to be true, it probably is! Good news consumers can recognize "fake news" that's spreading misinformation and confusing people. Understanding good sources will help you to identify real news. It's good to be informed!

GLOSSARY

accountable: Required to be responsible for something.

accuracy: How free something is of mistakes.

biased: Having a tendency to believe that some people or ideas are better than others.

credible: Reliable, believable.

document: A formal piece of writing.

ethical: Based on ethics, or rules based on what's right and what's wrong.

evaluate: To carefully judge the value of.

journalist: Someone who works with the collecting, writing, and editing of news stories for newspapers, magazines, websites, television, or radio.

media literate: Able to read, understand, and evaluate the many types of media you see every day; able to identify different types of media and understand their messages.

negative: About the real or supposed bad qualities of something or someone.

objective: Not influenced by personal feelings; based on facts.

technique: A method of accomplishing a task.

verify: To make sure something is true.

INDEX

WEBSITES

Due to the changing nature of Internet links, PowerKids Press has developed an online list of websites related to the subject of this book. This site is updated regularly. Please use this link to access the list: www.powerkidslinks.com/newslit/sources